A Scrappy Little Harvest

R. V. Bailey

Indigo Dreams Publishing

First Edition: A Scrappy Little Harvest
First published in Great Britain in 2016 by:
Indigo Dreams Publishing
24 Forest Houses
Halwill
Beaworthy
EX21 5UU

www.indigodreams.co.uk

ISBN 978-1-910834-28-2

British Library Cataloguing in Publication Data. A CIP record for this book can be obtained from the British Library.

Designed and typeset in Palatino Linotype by Indigo Dreams.
Cover design by Ronnie Goodyer at Indigo Dreams from Les Fauchiers by Julien Dupré

Printed and bound in Great Britain by 4edge Ltd
www.4edge.co.uk
Papers used by Indigo Dreams are recyclable products made from wood grown in sustainable forests following the guidance of the Forest Stewardship Council.

For U A Fanthorpe (1929-2009), who supplied the title.

Acknowledgements are due to the following:

Belgrave Press
Headland Press
Grey Hen Press
The Friend
The Friends' Quarterly
Wenlock Poetry Festival
Acumen
The Guardian
The Dark Horse

Also by R. V. Bailey:

Course Work
Marking Time
Credentials
From Me To You (with U A Fanthorpe)
The Losing Game
A Speaking Silence: Contemporary Quaker Poetry
(ed., with Stevie Krayer)
The Book of Love & Loss (ed., with June Hall)

CONTENTS

A Scrappy Little Harvest

A brief visit to London
Uncle Arly in Westminster Abbey: 12 May 2012

Hushed by the holy magnificence
Crowds shuffle and gaze;

Someone, glowing with private purpose,
Alone by a pillar kneels.

In Poets' Corner they gather with roses
To remember Edward Lear

And the complex clever man himself
Seems curiously near.

Blackbirds in early Bloomsbury twilight,
Squirrels in Russell Square;

The rare red kites climb vanishing high
In the home-going Oxfordshire air.

A poem for Peter Scupham

Pedagogue, poet, publisher,
Purveyor of books. Indeed
Four gentlemen at once, and –
Though none of them Cerberus –
All at the threshold.

The name is Go-between;
The vocation, Introduction.

Then to Now; the day
After yesterday to the day
Before tomorrow; the long-dead
To the not-yet-born. Here's

The true resurrection-man,
Calling to life the forgotten,
Obscure, misunderstood,
Investing them in words, wit,
And warmth.

It's courtesy; grace before meat;
Friendship practised over counties,
Centuries, in beloved Old Hall,
In a gardenful of Shakespeare
And donkeys.

Here is Peter, all his dear life
Seduced by poetry and people
And the fragile vigorous past:

Hooray for all four of him.

A song for the sun

Fickle the moon, whose light seduces;
Whose silver filigree touch reduces
All to black-and-white.

Dispassionate the distant stars,
Whose magic zodiac signs are snares
In the velvet night.

Only the truth-teller sun,
Honest as fire, sets light
To the spiders' lairs;

To the motes in the dancing airs,
And the stained-glass faraway
Field, fell, forest, bay.

Only the sun's strict finger will trace
Virtue and wrinkle and grace,
In a twilight face;

And alone the accurate sun will mark,
At the end of the long bright day,
The waiting dark.

After the party

A hot night, like this one. A sudden impulse, obeyed.
And half-an-hour's silence in a car, on top of a hill.

I suppose we felt need for air, after the party –
To get up high on a hill, from the stifling bowl of the town.

At the top of Cleeve we parked, to consider the view,
Though we didn't discuss it, or the night sky; or anything.

After sitting in silence one of us must have said
I suppose we ought to be getting back, and I drove you home.

Months later, I suppose it dawned on us together
Why we'd gone up the hill that night, and all that we didn't say.

An Old Inn Kitchen (Frederick William Elwell, 1870-1958)

He says us girls'll be the death of him
But that's not true. I seen the way he looks at us.
He's like my Dad was once, before
He went away to war and lost his wits
And Ma left home and all of us split up
And lucky me the only one of all of us
To get a berth like this. Me only twelve
When he took me on, that scared I was,
Homesick for Ma and all. He might of took
Advantage. There's many does.
He never.

They keep me young,
These Yorkshire lassies. Feather-headed,
Flighty, forgetful, the lot of them. But then:
They keep me on my toes. If Effie hadn't died
My own girls might have been their age.
I worry like a father. This place – I'm settled
Here, I like it. But there's dangers for a lass.
It's up to me to see they don't get into trouble,
To keep them safe. And train them up.
They'd get a place in service any day
With what I've taught them.

What happened to them once,
What might have happened since –
This moment on a sunny afternoon
Is all we have. And all we have
Is now – our past, like theirs,
Past, our future as unreal. Only
This moment, these friends, this sunshine,
This happiness. Now.

Archive

This is the temple of those who believe
In the future as well as the past.

Ordinary air is their incense, subtly conditioned;
Their liturgy devotion to detail, in whispers.

Among fading files, their deliberate demeanour is
Unhurried, as those who inhabit an eternal

Present. That their sacred charges might,
In the scheme of things, reveal themselves

Meaningless would be heresy, sacrilege,
Unimaginable. Worshippers in this

Shrine are the sanctioned, their credentials
Sobriety and faith, their state of grace

Avowed by scholars. Such votaries are
The angels of resurrection, who will call

These boxed and dusty back to life and breath,
Finding, in letters, in other men's' trivia,

The ligaments of everyday love that glows
Lively and bright as ever, and world without end;

That speaks the truth of yesterday and tomorrow;
That will outlast us all.

Await rescue

If it's safe to do so, you should stay
With your car.
And please advise us accurately
Where you are...

Sinking behind the trees, in the mist,
The sun's set the sky on fire. So I've guessed
That will be west.

A fine magnolia. In a garden, I'd say,
Though I see no house. It's roughly,
I suppose, a mile away.

Quite close, a throaty blackbird fills the night
Like a Wagnerian chorus. And on my right,

One cherry (pink), two blackthorns (white).
Under the dark hedge, dandelions
Glow in this magical half-light –

Gloaming, the Scots call it – (yes, I thought you were).

– You haven't found it *helpful*, what I've said?
But I've given you *facts*, can't actually *send* you this blur

Of bluebells, this garlic evening air.
From all I've told you, you must surely
Have *some* idea where...

Bear speaking

A cuddly old bear, that's me,
Furry, sentimental, kind.
A real soft touch. Soppy.
Avuncular, gentle. Mind

I see the way things ought to be,
How the whole job should go.
I like to get things right –
So don't tell me. I know.

These roars and snarls and teeth
Don't mean a thing, just toys,
It's how I am, a joker.
Just one of the boys.

A great big cuddly bear.
I'm a boss. But not a swine.
I'm looking after all of us,
Getting things in line.

You have to shout a bit
Or they don't hear.
A spot of the old adrenalin,
A touch of fear –

But it's all show.
I'm a pussy, a lamb.
Whatever you hear about me,
A cuddly old bear. That's who I am.

Or that's who I think I am.

'Be good, sweet maid, and let who will be clever'
(Charles Kingsley)

Fathers are the head of the family,
Said St Paul, taking his cue from analogy.
Fathers (unsurprisingly) agreed. Mothers,
Docile and practical, dealt with the butcher,
The grocer, the maids, and the money.

History does not regard them.

For us, it was our mothers who counted:
Who, before wedding bells in a riot
Of unthinking nosegays and hope,
Announced the clipping of wings,
Had tasted freedom; and remembered.

Sly as the filaments of buttercup roots,
They sowed in us notions of other futures.
They'd glimpsed lost chances, had noted how
Romantic starts shrink to serviceable ends:
How no proper work was proper for

The decent married, just child-birth, child-
Care; the baker's boy and the grocer's list.
And all the while seditiously they watched,
Dreaming dissenting futures while innocent fathers
Innocently turned the pages of *The Times*.

Matronly alchemy, mysterious as God, bore
In us at last the fruit their faith had sown.
We hold for each other the keys of the kingdom.
Sons need no locksmiths. But daughters – who knows
What keys, what doors, what futures may deliver

If good sweet maids should also find they're clever?

Birthday poem for 22 July

Since, in my foolish way,
I think of you each day,
How shall I celebrate
This singular date?

Friends you never met
Send cards for you, and yet
I who shared your life so long
Have no birthday song.

No gift, however treasure-trove,
Could represent my love;
A makeshift thing it was, although
You did not think it so.

Like everything you held
You turned it into gold –
Such alchemy that even I
Was made anew thereby.

All I can boringly find to say
On this your very special day
Hurray that you were ever born –
Hooray, hooray, hooray!

Botany lessons

What's that? you'd ask, pointing.
Yellow-rattle, I'd hazard; *Jack-
by-the-hedge?* Some I did know:
Yellow corydalis, that we hoped
Might colonise our walls, or
Wordsworth's favourite, *Lesser
Celandine,* that's already taken over.

My patient mother tried; but she
No more than you could fix in me
The names of flowers.

Now, climbing the lane,
I think of her, and you. And the
Flower names come back to me:
Moschatel, meadowsweet. Rue.

British Red Cross

Me, looking for digs, sent
By a kindly clergyman
To a west London square.

She, in the basement room,
Hoping I might take it. The rent,
The room, the afternoon – all gone

Except she was alone and what
She said: her friend was dead,
Her friend in the British Red Cross.

And that was her friend.
On the piano, framed.
Collared-and-tied.

Her uniform. Short hair,
Strong features. But it was more:
It was herself. It was her look –

The unashamed look of love.
Impossible, improper; wrong.
That was my friend,

She said, *My friend who died.*
Reluctant to hear and obscurely afraid,
I heard all that wasn't said.

I don't remember the afternoon
Or the room I might have taken.
But the friend. Not the name:

Just the face in the photo frame.
All in an instant, love's what I saw, and loss:
What had been, and was gone. The woman

In the basement; how it was for her, that day;
And how it was for me that day,
And how I ran away.

Brother Ass
(the name St Francis gave to his body)

Laughs aloud at the wrong moment.
Is hungry, insensitive, demanding;
Is in the way.

Is brave. Makes the dangerous
Important moves, dares to
Take the hand,

The heart. Understands precisely
The sacred magical geography
That is you.

But also steps back, runs away
Absurd, inelegant, just
When it shouldn't.

Rises to the challenge, falls
At the first fence. Means
To do better.

Obstinate, refuses the injunctions
Of grief and of despair,
Will not lie down

And die when it should; stands
At the pavement edge and waits
For the lights to change.

Mutinous, treacherous, lets out
Tears and howls at impossible
Moments, has no sense

Of decorum. Got us into this sweet mess
But has no idea where to go, what
To do now.

But

The hurt heart bleeds
Over the innocent supper table,
Over the last of the wine; and never
An eye for the clock.

Grieves for what was lost, and what
Was left behind; for yesterday,
Last month, a year ago. Before
Things hit the rocks.

Of course l love him still... But...

Ah, but.
A syllable that lies between
All that is love, and all that is not,
And all, perhaps, that it has never been.

Cautious

There are other conversations we might have had,
As we met on the hill: the one about Mr. Brown,
Or the new gate. But we talk about the weather,
As usual, and whether his washing will get wet.

There are other ways home I could have taken:
Through the houses, perhaps, or along the main road.
But I take the usual one, through the trees,
Down the hill where the blackberries grow.

Sometimes these bits of life, unspoken, unvisited,
Move shyly forward, as if their time has come.
We take a rougher road or talk of harder things.
The going's not so easy, but the views are good.

Yet further back again, some other time, the
Dark inconceivable, the vast unimagined
Lumbers towards the light, shouldering
Certainties aside, casting new shadows.

Christmas Poems

A Word from the Donkey

I found him in the manger with my hay.
Bald and without a tooth, helpless he lay;

There was no harm in him, so much was clear,
Not even I had anything to fear:

Castrated slave, patient and dumb and sad,
He saw me in his future, and was glad.

Bit parts

Not the stars: after so many
Christmas Eves familiar
As family, as shepherds, wise men,
Donkey, angels. We don't know

The innkeeper's views on that
Improvident lot in his stable. Or
Herod, at a distance, a spot
Of racial cleansing already in mind.

Someone's lining up tables
In the temple, the cash float ready
And the doves in cages. On the shore,
The decent puzzled fishermen;

The sickly, the tax-man; the shady
Lady and the touchy priests;
And Pontius Pilate's fractious missus
Can't get to sleep for nightmares.

Give it thirty years or so,
And somewhere somebody's
Already chopping down a tree
To be worked on later.

Striking the right note at Bethlehem

"... A birthday, yes, so what was needed
Was something festive, in a major key.
The party was a *most* impromptu thing,
No invitations – and no dress code: farm-

Hands in dungarees; foreign chaps, in suits –
Who brought some decent bottles. But
The venue – my dear, a stable! with *animals!*
At least they looked as if they felt at home.

The manger was a blessing. I didn't see
A midwife – though there must have been
One – none of the fellows I met there
Could have risen to that sort of thing..."

We still arrive with bottles, or flowers:
We're random and merry, unsure what to wear;
All of us trying to strike the right note,
And no one quite sure of the score.

Cistern song

In a cream-painted cupboard at the end of the bed
In my Grandma's room lived the cistern that fed

All the rest of the house. Her room, long and plain
And clean, was my chosen comfort zone,

Wide as a smile, warm as teacake, white as a cloud,
Crammed with stories and puzzles and dreams. We shared

The great white bed. And soothing, all night long,
The cistern's soliloquy, and Grandma's snoring song.

I was eight. My grown-up future was far away,
And all days with Grandma were holiday.

 I needed no other playmates: she alone was enough.
And steady as a rock in the background always
The cistern, doing its stuff.

Confused.com

What did he mean, the doctor,
On a scale of one to ten? And
Was it *an ache* or *a sharp pain*

Like a knife? He'd never been stabbed
Had no head for figures:
How could he know?

What did it mean, the thud
Of the heart in the night, the speck
Of dark on the handkerchief?

Talk of the elderly, of symptoms,
And the past. The others, the young,
They know: the price of everything,

The meaning of hashtag, algorithm.
Through them the future sneaks in,
Vivid, positive, with its calendar certainties

Tomorrow, October, next Christmas,
Their only past *last night*, or tedious
Holiday talk at dinner-tables.

This moment is so difficult. Like truth
Or love it won't be caught, slips
Through the fingers like soap in a bathtub.

Urgent, unsure, just sometimes
We try to grasp it, to hear what it's saying.
To know what it means.

Considering free love on St Mary's Island

– Would I talk about this with Dad?
You're joking! He wouldn't have a clue.

Seventeen, free-thinkers, sophisticated, us:
Love? *Free* love? Of course we knew.

On the island's springy turf we lay
Interrogating Life. We'd read such a lot:
We understood what was what.

How romantic it was; how inspiring the sea,
As twilight fell and the tide came in.
Going home, we were soaked to the knee.

Forty years on we begin to see
What we talked of then –
It was not love. And love is never free.

Daddy
(for Bill)

Daddy will be very cross. He
Will pull his hair out with both hands.

I never witnessed this phenomenon.
Perhaps I never was quite bad enough.

Our father, our mother: trying
In a difficult world to do it right.

The filaments of rage remain in you,
Dear brother, as they do in me –

Mere sparks beside his incandescent
Certainties, softened in us by

Mother's tranquil pragmatism, and
Her crosswords. I'm no good at wrath.

And I suspect, although you castigate
Yourself, my dear, that you're not

Happy with it either – you, helper,
Determined healer, maker-better;

Gentlest of confidants. We've lived
In a different world, and made

Our own mistakes, and understand regret.
I wonder did he ever feel misgivings?

Perhaps he did. Perhaps we should be
Sorry for him, now.

Dangerous times at the Writers' Centre

Watch your step here:
Not a room is safe.

A permanent resident's taken the sofa.
If she moves, a poem might die.

Papers are waiting for someone, quietly,
By the dining-room fire:

They're hotting up. Presently
A verse will ignite.

Even in the kitchen, where they
Minced up a shepherd for supper,

Metaphors bubble and squeak,
Rondeaux are rising.

Echoes in the garden,
Halloos to the reverberate hills –

Someone should be doing something,
Or where will it all end?

Dark

It is the nature of faith to be
dark. Whose place is not fireside
but promontory at night by winter sea.

Nor may you find it at Evensong,
most lovely of liturgies. It is out in the gale,
and alone, and nothing about it is safe.

It is where the rope frays on the rear-
ing crag, strung over tilting horizons,
where at finger's end only quicksilver

Love can find the cracks.

Disquiet in the countryside

Beware of the bull: I've just left him
In the field by the wood.
We hadn't expected to meet,
And that wasn't good:

His huge face loomed, curly and flat,
He made it clear how things stood.
We left it at that.

In the bush, a wren disguised as a leaf;
By the stream, a heron. In the lane
A rabbit washing whiskers. In the field a cow,
Fast asleep, indecorous legs all anyhow,
Innocent, vulnerable, dreamily lost.

I, who unwillingly frighten them all,
Wish I were a ghost.

The hedgerows observe, invigilate:
Belladonna-the-deadly, dispassionate,
And that triffid of the towpath,
Giant hogweed. Implacable, alert,

All they need to do is wait.

Druridge Bay

I can't remember being at Druridge Bay –
It was going that was important.
We might not get there, anyhow:
It might rain, or Father change his mind.

But going! The car's leather smell,
The bright blue drive, mile after mile
Down shimmering tarmac lanes.
                              At last, the sea –
Can you see it yet? – the magic line
Rising over coarse dune grass.

I could stand on the seat to gaze through the open roof
Or ride on the running-board
For the last few thrilling miles.

The silent engine's petrol smell in sunshine.
Father's first picnic cigarette.
Heaven about to happen.

Elocution lessons from Madame St John

What was he doing, the great god Pan,
Down in the reeds by the river?

Shyness the gag still, as it was then:
Eleven, being taught how to speak,
How to *speak up.*

Speak up, or you won't be heard.
But what to say? And will it be heard
Right? There were reasons for shyness,
For silence. When Madame had done with you
You could talk with anyone, however grand,
Talk *on the wireless,* even.

Slowly, silently, now the moon
Walks the night in her silver shoon.

The rhythm had power, and all those words
Beginning with S. (But *shoon?* Should
There be shoonshops?)

There are more reasons for silence now, and
More to say, though saying is fraught
With a different kind of danger. Every word
That escapes dissolves its misty truth
In saying, however many words you know.

Forget philosophy. Listen to the blackbird:
What he says is urgent. It has to do with food,
And love.

Ever after

He can boil an egg, can do
The shopping if she makes a list,
Knows how the washing-machine works.
Fine, he says, answering the phone,

We're absolutely fine. Upstairs
She's being sick again. The headache
Won't leave off. *Not my fault*, he thinks,
A man has a right to expect...

Not love but loneliness
Propelled them up the aisle.
He thought: *Other chaps have wives.*
We'll get along. She'll cook.

We'll make some friends. Do things.
And she: *Tweedy, like father.*
Strong. He'll know the ropes, take care,
Take on the rough for me.

They know each other better now,
And worse. Her nerves. His fear.
Their future like a shadow on the wall
Darkening daily.

Facing the music

Only the listener who loves
Has perfect pitch, can hear
The melody.

In the next room his mother attends
As he plays the difficult concerto
For the ninth time since breakfast.

Only she, her heart in time with his,
Can follow the intricate phrases
That Beethoven intended. As hard as he,

She practises her listening, has mastered
That *rallentando* in the Brahms,
And Mozart's unexpected change of key.

Falling

All over the world, this very minute,
They are falling. Ordinary people,
Just like you, are falling in love.

Tonight they will go home
To their chaste suburban beds
Different. A seismic shift.

They will sleep not at all,
All night. They will not dream
Or think. They will not care.

Tomorrow they will be the same
But not. They have suffered
Magic. A new world claims them:

Something they had supposed
Happened only to others
Has happened to them.

Tomorrow, in their everyday
Lives, they will talk sensibly.
Apparently, even, they may listen.

But their words are ritual,
A script. Themselves, they are
Somewhere else entirely.

Newspapers will not
Remark upon this, though it
Changes the world. You will

Notice, but you will not say.
When the gods take over
It is best to obey.

Fanny by gaslight

He was a sort of antimacassar man.
Meeting him, you thought of aspidistra,
Even gaslights. So when she blew into his life,

The windows rattled, the carpets
Lifted in the breeze, and suddenly
Nothing was quite itself any more.

Flowers in the cemetery

Ahead of me as always, you were first
To die. But what possessed you, love,
Trusting a feckless gardener like me
To plant the flowers on your grave?

It's garden-centre-best-suburban,
Sentimental, pink and blue,
Till in the natural course of things
I come to lie down here too.

Forget-me-nots and lavender –
What rustic clichés. Yes, I know:
I also know you will not care,
Since it was I who put them there.

Handbag
(for RF)

Flattened, rusty-black; a simple purse-like thing,
Seventy years old, or more. How is it still
Here, after so many years, so many lives?

No handkerchief, no perfume, letters:
Its mute emptiness aches. I like to think
He gave it you, your son who loved you.

How close you were, just mother and child;
Such savagely censorious times. *Contra
Mundum*, in disgrace. And I like to think

How both of you enjoyed it later when,
His wife and kids abandoned for a week,
The two of you eloped, alone.

His pocket diary's here; it's black, as well.
The eloquent barrister's writing inside
Brimming with grief the day you died.

Harold

There must have been a pair of trousers
Somewhere along the line.

Harold, you see, was a very public man:
Not for him the soubriquet *loner*.

In other places they'd have strung him up,
Castrated him, or tarred and feathered.

Here the police just *had a word*, about
The shortness of his skirts, and

Hanging about too near the school.
Here he got away with being different.

We all learnt from him – the vicar,
Even the bishop – and probably God –

That difference can be dear. To be cared for,
To be welcomed, to be grateful for.

Harry
(for Harry Chambers, 1937–2012)

Above the sheet and the oxygen mask,
The untamable black lick of hair, the
Wide-open eyes. The same sixth-former
Who's just got another bright idea.

Harry. Who knew all the poets, knew
The *very-man-for-the-job*, who
Never forgot a line. Who could quote
Us all silent till midnight and after.

O Harry – the room was full. The poets there.
The launch you'd so carefully fixed
Began without you. Then crash in the midst
Of some timid stanza, the last to arrive,

You – with a box of books far bigger than you
And the wrong trousers (*the train was late,
There wasn't a cab, don't stop for me*) –
Who afterwards swept us all away

To *the best place there is round here
For miles.* And picked up the bill. Harry:
Who fought for our innocent words
With London men in suits, across mahogany.

Harry. The man who took a chance on us,
Who opened the cage, let the birds free to sing.
Who'd shut Harry out of any
Half-decent heaven? Let the party begin.

In Costa

It must have been poetry.
I can't account for it in any other way.
In London you don't expect it.

We can all talk about the weather
So that's what we discussed –
The chanciness, the need to be prepared

For rain, light rain or downpour,
For tropical heat, and stations in between.
I was prepared for weather, and

Perhaps it was my brolly on the table.
I wasn't prepared for him, a stranger,
Stopping to talk as he was leaving:

In London you don't expect it.
Had I met him before? Should I know him –
This entirely agreeable stranger?

But I think it was probably the book –
The book I was reading. A poetry book.
Shamelessly, in Costa.

Infestation

Field mice, over the years,
We've had, and banished
Humanely in the adjacent
Churchyard, fearing
They might nest in the piano.

Mostly our dragons are benign:
Their toothpaste grins,
Their twinkly painted eyes –
Doris, in the bathroom,
Custard (among the roses).

The other dragons, progeny
Of the worm, are vile.
They're alien, not tame:
They have no names;
They do not smile or play.

They never go away

In the garden

Poppies that you loved so much
Glow in the dark borders
With their old oriental purpose.

Tame blackbirds that you liked
Nourish nestfuls of young
On Waitrose sultanas.

The garden gets on with itself
As gardens do, and the church
Bells echo everywhere,

Even over the blackbird, ruthless knave,
That tears the young heads off the poppies
I planted on your grave.

Last house

No good looking back, he says,
Wistfully, marooned with the *Telegraph*
In his comfortable chair. His wife
Likes it here, so much storage space
In the kitchen, such a view
From the garden.

The view from the garden, wide
And lovely, changes delightfully
As the seasons change. But his
Morning strolls down the High Street, his
Amiable neighbours... *Must look forward,*
That's the thing.

He folds the paper. Climbs out
Of the comfortable chair, pads round
Their carefully-designed eminently suitable
Quarters, considers the view from the garden,
The hill they'll have to climb to get him
In the end.

Learning in the Library

He is teaching me to swim.
It is November. There are leaves
On the pool, and no one in it but me.

A huge strong bear of a man,
He is my boss, and he tells me

I must learn to swim – although
It is my lunch-hour, and he knows
That in the afternoon I will fall asleep,
And bibliography may suffer.

Apparently this does not matter.
It is nineteen fifty-four, and the Library
A civilised place, with its own priorities.

Winter comes on. Despite his efforts,
I never learn to swim. Instead I master
The Russian alphabet, command of which
Is the first step towards cataloguing
Our Russian Acquisitions. So now
I fall asleep over title pages in Cyrillic.

On other afternoons, setting aside the needs
Of seventeenth century pamphlets
In the remoter regions of the Library,
A gifted young colleague feels drawn
To introduce me, in compelling detail,
To the idiosyncratic delights
Of the railway system at Peterborough.

I never forgot the Library. Nothing
In the dry years that followed ever matched
Such a lofty and disinterested view of learning.

Life-drawing at New Park: group portrait

The usual suspects; and me – a bit
Late, a bit reluctant – passing
No Entry signs, the well-fed
Sheep, the peacocks. The marble hall.

Angus is tall, touchy, gruff;
In orange shorts. Terse lines
From nose to mouth mean
Shut up. We're here to work.

The model, in familiar
Regrettable shades of sludge;
His dog, shut in the car,
Wails *affetuoso*. From the kitchen

The parrot's jungle whoops. A shower
Of expensive gravel: Judy's Volvo.
And she in neat black almost-cocktail number,
Her easel with too many legs and a mind of its own.

We settle. *At last*, thinks Angus.
Peacock and parrot shriek. The model
Calms us with his tranquil presence.
This is the job. To catch them all,

Clothes, feelings, voices off.

Morning prayer C21

The person you are calling knows you are waiting

O Lord, who hast safely brought us
to the beginning of this day,

Your call is important to us

Defend us in the same with thy mighty power;

Do not hang up, caller

And grant that this day we may fall
into no sin, neither run
into any kind of danger,

We are trying to connect you

but that all our doings may be
ordered by thy governance
to do always that is righteous in thy sight

The person you are calling knows you are waiting

My mother deals with a case of *Vestibule Paralysis*

Which is the malady of the departing guest:
Reluctant to leave, with another *By-the-way*,
Another *I forgot to tell you...*

                              Well, Frank,
My mother would say, *we must go to bed.*
These good people will be wanting to go home.

No, she didn't say it. But she might have,
My tactless, warm-hearted, witty mother.

Stepmother's breath out there, she'd say, after
Dancing down the garden to bring the washing in,
The sea wind chill on her face. *Put the kettle on,*
Sweetheart, let's have a bit of comfortable.

She had a crossword-solver's cleverness,
The sturdy footings of an old-style grammar-school,
An insatiable appetite for books.

She'd have liked to be able to sing – Bach,
Handel, not just *The Methodist Hymnbook.*

Still game at ninety-five, we'd hear her
Oh, for the wings, for the wings of a dove,
Far away, far away would I rove... with
Operatic conviction, in the bath.

Her contempt for Hitler; the way
She took it for granted I could cope with anything,
With our flashpoint electric plugs, with the mad
Neighbour who wanted to walk into the sea.

She admitted that I couldn't do algebra.

But what she was – her laughter,
Her persistent kindness; her wartime jokes
And random serious speculations, even her
Inspired austerity cooking – taught me
What I knew of love.

And she was always there.

We were on holiday, thinking her safe
In the care of friends, when she decided
It was time. Unselfish as ever, she didn't say
That she had it in mind to die. She didn't
Talk about her faith, caught from her father
As easily as his looks.

Yet this is how, if we ever do,
We come across God: in his lookalike people,
Casual in high street or hospital, who have
Perfect pitch in the art of being human.

North Sea, 1940

Barbed wire was one thing: torn gym-slips testified
To its intricate weave. As it rolled along the cliff-top,
Sharp and shining, it might have slowed him down.

The sea was another thing entirely.

Not dainty like the Channel, it foamed
Four hundred miles (we knew) to the other side,
To *Schleswig-Holstein*. With Hitler
Probably, impatient on the shore.

Was it the sea that stopped him? It wasn't our guns.
While searchlights fingered the dark a whole street vanished.

The sea spoke, all night long, hushing against the shore.
The beach was *Out of bounds*. The cliffs *Out of bounds*.
Who cared? But the sea told tales to my mother
Through my shoes with their tide-line of salt.

The sea, grey-green, like a German uniform;
Was chill, familiar, seductive; more real than Hitler.

Daily the sea swallowed the horizon, daily
It savaged our bit of England. Unlike Hitler
It always knew when to stop.

Notes from the old dons

I do not seem to have received
an essay from you this week.
Am I mistaken, or is this so?

Of course it was so. But how
courteous they were, the old dons.

I expect the seventeenth and eighteenth
century papers suffered from
the general settling down process...

So much more generous than
Too many sherry parties in
the Michaelmas Term.

I am very pleased with your place
in the Tripos (writes the Dean), *knowing*
what a field of battle Paper 1A is...

'A field of battle.' Considering
all the things he might have said.

We weren't there to be taught, but
To learn. We worked; or slacked. Perhaps
We tried. I hope at least we learnt their tact.

Orchid

Arrives like a grandee, with a retinue;
Postman, baffled by fierce orders –
Protect from extreme heat or cold;

Like a princess, shielded
From us and our dingy world
By great wrappings of

Expanded polystyrene;
Each petal of each plant
Swathed by itself, in tissue.

Ah! What fine lady's-maid fingers
Have tended all this! How it looms
Above our humble indoor plants –
Our Christmas cactus. Our cyclamen.

Painting Tinker

I wouldn't do it like that today,
The painter said, looking at
His picture of our boat.

What he meant was:
I know better now. I know that
What you see's not how it is. I see
Things like an artist now, post-
Modern. We artists understand
What's really there.

But faithful to its greens and browns,
That's how it looked to us. We felt
At home with it. After all,
We'd lived there: primitives,
Inside his painting.

Piano

Like having a piano in the house
We all need someone on whom to practise
Love. Arpeggios of passion, chords of content,

Persistent scales of care, with sharps or flats.
Not necessarily the great concerto
Of long-established wedded partnership –

Short practice pieces, over telephones,
To solitary friends; quick suburban trills
In shopping mall or high street;

Cadenzas in airmail envelopes
For dears Down Under.
But practise, practise. That's the thing:

Beethoven sonatas can't be achieved
In a week. Unpractised fingers of love
Won't be sure or supple enough

When a concert performance is urgently needed
For child, father, friend, neighbour,
Stranger, enemy.

Programme notes

The tickets all went at least a month since.
The hall is full, and hushed, and dark. The orchestra
Is taut with purpose, sixty instruments leashed

To the conductor's eyebrow. *Pianissimo, adagio,* the merest
Hint of the first subject. The figure at the keyboard
Is an extension of the keyboard. And as still, until

Soloist, strings, woodwind and brass all in together,
Each muscle tuned to the visceral pitch
Of a man two hundred years dead.

Appassionato the pianist leans, his fists
Invisibly producing cadenzas. In the stalls
His mother notes: *He's got it, that tricky E flat.*

Rather further back, in his usual seat,
With his usual acerbity, the reviewer compares
This fellow's interpretation with Tuesday's man.

And high in the last-minute seat of the gods
His future listens. She believes every note he strikes
Comes direct from heaven.

Quaker Funeral
(for Mary and Frank)

Outside, the daughters stand in cold sunlight.
We all get hugs. *Thank you for coming.*
Muffled in miscellaneous grief we trail inside;
Stand, when her coffin comes, then fold ourselves
Quietly back, watching our shoes, or closing eyes.

Silence.

At the back, somebody gets up and speaks.
I'm lucky to have known them.

Silence.

Somebody reads a poem by MacNeice.

Silence.

The old man clambers upright, wheezing,
Handkerchief, glasses, white stick
Clutched like resolution. Important things
Are trying to get said through a voice
On the edge of howling.

I miss them...when my wife died...
Tears are winning. He won't let them.
They came every day...one or the other
Choke. We wait, out of our depth.
Came to see me...kept me going...

Silence.

Latecomers as we were, we didn't add our ha'porth:
Long before we knew her name, and after, too,
Between ourselves we called her *Celia Johnson.*
For her beauty, wit, and a kind of shining.

Queen
(for FRM)

She is not like us. She is queen.
You may imagine the courtiers
Moving like unspoken thoughts
To purify, polish, arrange

The scenery, before she enters.
Taller than we are, the air she breathes
Is pure; and rather colder
Than the rest of us relish.

Her words are ours, it's true,
But in their Sunday best: not *bikes,*
But *motor-bicycles;* not *farm* but
Agricultural workers. No *guys*

Or *blokes* exist: just *gentlemen,*
Or *honest folk,* all *fine upstanding*
Fellows, just this side of dashing.
Not a shifty eye or a wink among them.

How royal the world, if only
It were true. At least she did her bit
To raise the game; patrician that she was,
She never let us down.

Seven years on: 28.04.16

Floor becomes air as trapdoor opens –
Abrupt and imperative as the hangman's
Drop. Seven years on: and I'm still shaken,
As speechless now as I was then.

Seven years hard have taught me how
To jack-in-the-box, come back again
To the flat landscape of ordinary days,
Where no one remembers how it was.

But I remember. It is like this always:
Nameless, countless those whose loves,
Whose children, fathers, lives

Lie in the roadside dust, or under the sea,
Their dear futures cancelled; or who

Are rubble beneath the masonry
Of a fallen town; or fester on
After bullet and shrapnel have long since gone.

Hearts are breaking all the time;
There's nothing very special about mine.
Grief cries uncomforted, and armies mass
World-wide. And centuries pass.

Silver Band

Is best heard from a distance.

Uniforms show it's a serious undertaking;
And their stern striding, their great tramping feet.

Reliable as ground-bass their gentle hoots
Their honking and tweeting; an assembly of owls

Perhaps – for how can human mouth
Contrive such orchestration?

Their voiceless conductor watches: his charges
Alert, sucking their lips, instruments at the ready;

The farmer just back from the field, embracing
His French horn and its astonishing innards;

The soloist with her innocent fragile face,
Her high heels, her body still with anxiety,
Waiting her turn among these vast bell-mouthed flowers

Whose deeply frivolous, deeply serious,
Deeply vulgar Judy Garland sounds are
Always on the verge of a raspberry. Who

Get nearer the heart than any orchestra.

Song at harvest time
Omnia pro pecunia facta sunt

Man, mad for mastery,
Splitting the bone from the blood,
The flower from the field,
The tree from the wood.

A light wind that morning,
Under the wide Yorkshire sky, and
Someone has left a couple of roses
By the cross. The mild fields around us
Are wheat-sown, impassive.

It was springtime when we came
To Towton. Five hundred years ago,
It was almost April, too, but that
Dark morning was winter still: snow,
And a whirling wind that whooped
The arrows. All day long they were at it,
Stopping only to shovel the shambles aside
So they could make more dead. Cut down
As they fought face to face, trampled
Into messes as they ran; drowned
In the river as they fled. Afterwards,
How the innocent fields stank.

Their women, left behind –
What of them, with no tall fellow
To hold the tail of the plough?
No one writes of them.

Man, mad for mastery,
Splitting the bone from the blood,
The flower from the field,
The tree from the wood.

At Wharram Percy, the passionless turf.
We couldn't imagine how it had been,
Till a low sun cast impressions on the land
And the shadows came alert.

Not cold steel: it was cold hearts there,
Avarice, and the profits off sheep,
And plague, always at hand to pick clean
When men run out of novel ways to kill.

Easier to be lined up by a trench,
And shot in the head; quicker
To be shot in the back by a sniper
On a Damascus roof. All deaths
Are black, and usually at the end
A filthy muddle and a vile smell.

The hedges are torn down now, the fields
Endless, world-wide, fed by centuries
Of mortal compost. So many so casually dead.
What harvest will come home to those who wait
Wanting only a quiet hearth and bread?

Man, mad for mastery,
Splitting the bone from the blood,
The flower from the field,
The tree from the wood.

The Battle of Towton was fought during the Wars of the Roses on 29th
March 1461.

Sister-in-law
(Diary entry, 15. 08. 80: *Alas! Joan goes.*)

You missed your vocation, Joan.
A talent for friendship, for letter-writing,
Travel, talk (both narrative and argument) –
Nature meant you for a Paris *salon*
In some interestingly turbulent time.

Elegant, intolerant, intransigent, kind,
Intractable, impractical, vivacious, brave,
Generous, impetuous, impossible woman:

Touchy explorer who ventured further
Than any of the rest of us – taker-on
Of lame dogs, lost souls, hopeless causes –
These words are for you, Joan.

                    Rest quiet now.

Statutory Man

Imagine when our time comes,
The Statutory Man. How we shall pet him,
The darling, with his curls and his long
Legs; and pay no attention at all
To anything he says.

Of course he will get together
With other darlings, since they are so few,
And gossip about the things men
Care about, that really don't signify,
Like money, and football.

How gladly we'll depend on them
To do the clearing up and office chores;
To remember boring details, manicure
Our urgent diaries, book our flights, our
Suitable accommodation.

Their elegance. Their selfless readiness
To represent one half the human race
Without expecting more than dinner out
Occasionally, wine; a bit of orchestrated
Flattery and flirting in a cab.

It's not quite happened yet. But soon
They'll understand how things should be:
Gladly they'll move from centre stage
And leave us girls to get on making
Everything all right again.

Terminal ward

So close a conspiracy, only the doomed
Know this club exists; and membership
Costs all you have.

Passwords are few. They are easily mastered.
Of course there are rules: you must expect
No concessions.

Comrades are random, unsuitable, un-chosen:
Strangers washed up on a life-raft in
Uncharted seas.

You hear what they utter, may even yourself
Confide. But remember the envoy
Who brought you here,

Who knows you well, is by your side, is
Eager to advise. His name is Death.
He holds your breath.

The Banker's Tale

Portly and powerful,
The old-fashioned kind.

Secure behind secretary
And clutter-free mahogany:
Fat pen in firm hand
Cancelling the hopes of lesser men.

Secure in the scheme of things:
Smug amid brandy
And carefully calibrated
Business-men's jokes.

One night
Coming home
Ran over a cat.

He'd hardly feel it. Nothing
To him, you'd think,
In his big quiet car.

His costly tan turned white,
He couldn't eat. Was sick,
Brought low. Next day
He couldn't go to work.

Human nature being what it is
It seems even a banker needs
Bayonet-practice, battle-cry, drill
Before he can comfortably kill.

The little wood

There's always a little wood somewhere
Where you think of what lies ahead:
Meeting the hostile client;

Chairing the difficult Board;
Breaking the dreadful news.
You wonder how you got here,

When almost anyone you've ever known
Would do a better job; you think
How very much you'd like to get away.

In the wood, you seem to have a choice.
Briefly you're Machiavelli.
Strategic illness calls.

In the little wood you learn the cost,
And why you're there. And who
You are. And what, in fact, you'll do.

The readiness is all

The End – belongs to
Credits, in the cinema:

For us, the daily diaries,
Not the Twin Towers.

Continuity is what we deal in;
The next step, not The Life.

The unknown that's more
Reliable than the known

Waits for us after the pips.
Listening's the mode,

The will to hear: a child
Seen, not heard, alert

To cues from wherever,
Whatever the idiom.

Like balancing across
Niagara: high and

Afraid, in a mode
Ineffable, numinous,

Absolute.

Tidying

How we'd relish talking about all this.
One day, together again, we'll find
The holiday side of nightmare.

1. I'm irrelevant here, yet I can't let go.
You'll never wake again, I know –
I'll not say *Tea? I've brought us tea,*
As I used to, mornings after gigs,
Carefree on jumbo beds at anonymous inns
All over England.

Heart's the last thing going, and gallantly
Won't give up. The rest of you
Signed off days ago.

Your body's been out to get you
From the start: *If they're small as this*
We usually throw them back (the doctor,
The day you were born). Since then
It's been telling you, again and again,
How right he was.

These days, these nights: a tedious
Journey that at last leads home
To a broken home; where
Somehow fragments will have to be sorted,
Somehow assembled, somehow
Redeemed.

From time to time procedures must take place.
Which, they say, I shouldn't see. (*True:*
I have supped full of horrors already,
Watching your last night's fever.)
Meekly I leave, haunt corridors.
Find coffee.

2.   The morning nurses have re-organised you,
Have left you, arms stretched on the sheet,
Something between Brueghel
And a tombstone knight. Your lower teeth
Gleam, strange in your mouth's gloom.
Can you not make her look – more at ease?

Ah, sorry! It's a nursey thing, they say, *to be tidy.*
We'll turn her on her side.

Under the sheet, under
The crisp folds of the hospice sheet
Your hand's in mine. For my comfort,
Probably, warm, engaged as ever;
Yet maybe also for yours,
Who dreaming deep may need my hold
To steady you on your road.

My love, you are turning to
Compost now. Something, perhaps,
Good for roses, or poppies.

Time to move on to God.

3. Your breathing's bubble
And squeak drowns the April
Evening blackbird, will at last
Drown you. I pour a solitary *fino*
From the bottle we shared
While you still could swallow,
Toast your courage, your dear
Simplicity, your final
Leap into life.

Well-brought-up women don't cry. I tuck
The bits of my heart in my pocket,
Tidily; and remember to
Say thank you to the nurse.

Tightrope

'Where comedy fails, what we have is misery, not tragedy.'

(Iris Murdoch)

Razor's edge; tight, strait.
On one side grow platitudes,
Facetiousness, banality.

A host of self-serving beasts
Roam its margins, affable,
Ingratiating.

The thin line is called Fool.

Fool is acceptable. Hoping
It will bear my weight
I edge along it, timidly.

Underneath is the dark.

To be let furnished

There are no books. But
The furniture is eloquent:

How ill at ease that sofa,
Sick for some bright showroom.

The bits and pieces from well-meaning friends
Refuse their vocation; mournful castaways,

They know they are not wanted, cannot settle
Comfortably, even with each other:

They hanker for the attic, where they belong.
Or the tip. On the shelf, shepherd and

Shepherdess are spaced exactly,
Not looking at each other.

Newspaper lines the kitchen drawers.

Try harder

That you have died is a pity.
Perhaps. After all, you were guilty
Of a number of morbidities. We accuse you
Of colonic polyps; of bi-polar depression;
Of pernicious anaemia; and of that plausible
Set of symptoms known as chronic fatigue.

You were also a woman of a certain age.

You should have known better than to come
To us, specialists as we are at sprains and rashes,
Cuts and bruises, problems easily diagnosed
That respond obediently to treatment
(Also anything interesting or glamorous,
Like heart attacks or sudden death).

But you were just a woman who was tired.

Everybody's *tired*. I am tired. You just don't try.
I've examined you. You say the swelling hurts?
You can't do up your trousers? Well, lose weight.
In my surgery I have people who are *really ill*.
You don't need a scan or another opinion –
Just pull yourself together. Get out more.

So now you are a woman who is dead.
Pity. We did say we'd support you.

You could have tried harder.

West Side Story
(with apologies to Stephen Sondheim)

Sounds like something lost.
It wasn't lost on us.

The song was a popular song,
With a far-from-original theme.
That night it was sung along

In a sixties film, schemed
From a fifties Broadway
Show, a musical suggested by

Juliet and Romeo, whose plot
Shakespeare'd got
From an old Italian yarn

That other men had English'd
(into prose and verse) some years
Before the Stratford Bard

Was even born. There now.
What a tale. As I said,
Far from original.

But what a tale. And even then
In the up-to-date cinema dark
Not the least bit stale.

Neither of us had words to guess
What might lie ahead of us,

Only the word *somewhere*
Somehow suggesting a place in the air;
In the bright air.

Who's Fleur, then?
(for Fleur Adcock)

How can I begin?

        In the middle.
You can't return to the start.

It was never about safety.
How could it be, when
What you write about is always
On the point of disappearing?

She's one for the edge, for accident,
Coincidence, surprise. Fleur and the
Poem? Accomplices. You could never
Use the word predictable.

A woman with an appetite
For hills. An eye for what's
Distinctive in a landscape,
In a bird, a person; an ear for
Words, accents, intonations –
And what's left out.

So how did she do it?

Upright, head-on. Thought-
Through. By listening. By taking it
Seriously. By handing it out when done
With its socks pulled up and its laces
Tight as a drum.

How did it sound? You did say
She had an ear.

        Patrician, then:

Bone-china, flicked with a fingernail
In autumn dusk. But kinder,

Finding the scenic route through
Him and her, in the suburbs, in the
Everyday. In the net of the stars.

You couldn't tell she was a poet?

You wouldn't guess. There was
No looking in the mirror. Nothing
Ingratiating, no festival antics.

The inner eye is not amenable
To dissection.

       I told you, stars:
Upward was where she looked.
The laughter (O there was laughter)
Was clever. Could be wild; could
Be merciless. Never hurt.

So – what am I to make of her,
At eighty?

       What she always was:
Nobody's fool. A nightingale.

Words, words, words

The neighbours are kind, and relieved
That I wind the clock and feed the birds,

That I'm clean and respectably dressed,
And not at a loss for words.

Shyly they ask how I'm feeling.
Oh, better, you know, getting there.

(Out of the question to speak the truth:
Damaged beyond repair.)

Words have lost their piquancy,
They're treacherous as weather;

Ours, for instance, or *yours* and *mine,*
Or *happy.* Or *together.*